INSIDE THE INDUSTRY
SPORTS

BY BRIAN HOWELL

INSIDE THE INDUSTRY

BY BRIAN HOWELL

Content Consultant
Warren Whisenant, PhD
Associate Chair, Department of Kinesiology & Sport Sciences
Sport Administration Program, University of Miami

ABDO
Publishing Company

CREDITS

Published by ABDO Publishing Company, 8000 West 78th Street, Edina, Minnesota 55439. Copyright © 2011 by Abdo Consulting Group, Inc. International copyrights reserved in all countries. No part of this book may be reproduced in any form without written permission from the publisher. The Essential Library™ is a trademark and logo of ABDO Publishing Company.

Printed in the United States of America,
North Mankato, Minnesota
112010
012011

Editor: Chrös McDougall
Copy Editor: David Johnstone
Interior Design and Production: Christa Schneider
Cover Design: Christa Schneider

Library of Congress Cataloging-in-Publication Data
Howell, Brian, 1974-
  Sports / by Brian Howell.
      p. cm. -- (Inside the industry)
  Includes bibliographical references.
  ISBN 978-1-61714-804-0
  1. Sports--Vocational guidance--Juvenile literature. I. Title.
  GV734.H68 2011
  796.023--dc22
                                        2010042558

TABLE OF CONTENTS

Michael Jordan hit the winning shot to give the Chicago Bulls a victory in the 1998 NBA Finals.

IS A SPORTS JOB FOR YOU?

"Sport is where an entire life can be compressed into a few hours, where the emotions of a lifetime can be felt on an acre or two of ground, where a person can suffer and die and rise again on six miles of trails through a New York City park. Sport is a theater

where sinner can turn saint and a common man become an uncommon hero, where the past and the future can fuse with the present. Sport is singularly able to give us peak experiences where we feel completely one with the world and transcend all conflicts as we finally become our own potential."
— *author George A. Sheehan*[1]

It was Game 6 of the 1998 National Basketball Association (NBA) Finals. The crowd at the Delta Center in Salt Lake City, Utah, was on its feet. Time was running out. The hometown Utah Jazz held an 86–85 lead.[2] A win would push the series to a decisive Game 7. But Michael Jordan had the ball.

The Chicago Bulls guard had made big shots before, but there was no bigger shot than this. Jordan dribbled on the left side of the court, waiting for the clock to tick down. Then, with ten seconds remaining, he made his move. Jordan rushed to the right and then stopped, faked out Jazz defender Byron Russell, and put up a jump shot.

Swish.

Just like that, the Bulls won 87–86. It was the sixth NBA title in eight years for Jordan, the Bulls, and Chicago.[3] And like so many times before, Jordan was the hero.

Around the country and around the world, millions of fans watched on TV and listened on the radio as Jordan delivered another great moment in sports. Pulitzer Prize-winning author George F. Will once wrote, "Sports serve society by providing vivid examples of excellence."[4] Jordan's shot was another example of excellence.

SPORTS IN OUR CULTURE

"People understand contests. You take a bunch of kids throwing rocks at random and people look askance, but if you go and hold a rock-throwing contest—people understand that."[5]

— *Don Murray, executive secretary of the United States Surfing Association*

Many kids watch athletes like Jordan and dream of being a professional athlete, too. And who wouldn't? They get paid—sometimes millions of dollars—to play a game, and fans around the world adore them. But very few people ever become professional athletes. It takes a rare combination of natural ability, hard work, and a little bit of luck to reach that level. However, while the athletes are the stars of the show, you don't need a uniform to be an important player in the sports industry.

Go back to the Delta Center in Salt Lake City. Let's freeze on that moment when Jordan hit his amazing shot. It was Jordan, of course, who provided that great moment in sports history. But, have you ever considered the other people who helped make that moment a reality? In addition to Jordan and the other players, the Delta Center was filled with people working and fulfilling their dreams of having careers in the sports world.

A SURVEY OF SPORTS JOBS

Along with the players, each team had coaches who guided the players throughout the season. On the court, three referees made sure the players followed the rules. Most coaches and referees work their way up to that point. Many spend years working at the high school, college, or minor league level before reaching the NBA.

Taking care of the players before, during, and after the game were team doctors and trainers. These men and women had gone to school for medical degrees and were responsible for making sure the players were healthy enough to get on the court.

Seated near the court were dozens of sportswriters. They watched the players with a careful eye and took notes about the action so they could write stories about the game. Their responsibility was to tell the story of the game, putting their readers in that moment.

Near the sportswriters were dozens of radio and TV broadcasters—men and women who provided the commentary and insight for the millions watching or listening to the game at home. While the broadcasters were the ones seen on television and heard on the radio, a team

PLENTY OF OPTIONS

Comedian Jay Leno once quipped, "I wanted to have a career in sports when I was young, but I had to give it up. I'm only six feet tall, so I couldn't play basketball. I'm only 190 pounds, so I couldn't play football. And I have 20–20 vision, so I couldn't be a referee."[6]

Leno was, of course, looking for a laugh. But, for those who are serious about a career in sports, the options are seemingly limitless. The sports industry is not just for athletes.

of technicians worked behind the scenes to produce the final product.

Each sports team also had the men and women who were responsible for building and running the team. The team owner wrote the checks and made some of the bigger decisions. The general manager and his or her assistants made choices as to which players to sign to contracts, which college players to select in the draft, or which players to obtain in trades.

In order to find the players to sign, the teams had to hire scouts—people who evaluate talented players from all corners of the globe. These scouts spend countless hours in gyms and at fields watching young athletes and deciding whether they have the ability to play as professionals.

The teams also had men and women working in public relations, community relations, marketing, and advertising—all with the common goal of promoting the team. Other staff

SPORTS CAREERS IN FILM

There are dozens of sports movies, many of them celebrating the accomplishments of teams or athletes. But there are also several films that center on different sports careers. The 1996 film *Jerry Maguire* is about a sports agent for high-profile athletes. The 1991 film *Talent for the Game* follows a scout as he searches for major league baseball talent. Josh Hartnett and Samuel L. Jackson star in *Resurrecting the Champ*, a 2007 film that gave some insight into the life of a sports journalist. Other movies, such as *Hoosiers* and *Glory Road*, feature basketball coaches as main characters and show some of the duties they have in their careers.

Referees, umpires, and other officials are needed to officiate organized sports at all levels.

members were responsible for selling tickets and keeping season-ticket holders happy. Still others managed the team's stadium, making sure the players and fans had everything they needed.

Without all of these people, Jordan's game-winning shot during the 1998 NBA Finals would not have been the remarkable moment it was. Jordan didn't need all those people to help him make a great shot, but without them, who would have known about it?

Jordan was one of the lucky few who had what it takes to realize his dream of becoming a professional athlete.

KNOW YOUR BUSINESS

Mike Krzyzewski is the men's basketball coach at Duke University and for the US men's national team. He is one of the most successful college coaches of all time. Coach K didn't get to where he is by simply knowing how to coach basketball. "A common mistake among those who work in sport is spending a disproportional amount of time on x's and o's as compared to time spent learning about people," he said.[7]

But, when you dream of a career in sports, remember that the sports world is filled with a variety of options. This book will take an inside look at how to get into the sports world by examining four careers in the industry: professional athlete, sports agent, college coach, and sportswriter. Each one of these careers is unique in the skills required and the path to get there.

TEN POPULAR SPORTS JOBS

1. **Professional athlete:** Athletes are the stars of the show. They are the players who compete in the sporting events.

2. **Sports agent:** Agents help ensure that the athletes have to worry only about the games. They handle the athletes' non-sports dealings, such as contract negotiations and endorsement deals.

3. **College coach:** A college coach has two primary roles. One is to guide the players in games and practices. The other is recruiting new players to join the team.

4. **Sportswriter or other journalist:** Journalists keep the fans updated on their favorite teams. They attend practices and games and write about what is happening so that fans are always in the know. Other journalists broadcast their reports on TV or radio.

5. **Professional scout:** With so many athletes in the world, and so few openings on professional team rosters, scouts travel the world and ensure that their team signs the best players.

6. **Sports information director:** Sports teams are filled with information. The sports information director works with journalists to ensure that the team's news and message get to the public.

7. **Athletic director:** College athletics departments often have many teams, each with their own players, coaches, and support staff. The athletic director manages everyone.

8. **Sports marketing agent:** In a career that combines business skills and sports knowledge, a sports marketing agent helps find sponsorship deals, promotes events, and performs other duties to ensure the team or event is visible to the public.

9. **Team trainer/doctor:** All professional athletes experience injuries or aches and pains from time to time. Trainers and doctors help the athletes recover from those injuries so they can get back on the field quicker.

10. **Stadium/arena manager:** The stadium manager is responsible for making sure the facility is safe at all times for athletes, coaches, and fans.

Athletic trainers help athletes stretch and avoid injuries.

Kobe Bryant won his fifth **NBA** title with the Los Angeles Lakers in 2010. He is a sports star who is known around the world.

WHAT IS A PROFESSIONAL ATHLETE?

If you have ever thought about becoming a professional athlete, you have most likely envisioned a career that includes fame and fortune. You may have imagined yourself making all-star teams and producing amazing plays. You've also probably imagined yourself buying exotic cars and homes with all the money you're making.

While all that is possible, it is important not to focus your career goal on becoming the next Kobe Bryant, Derek Jeter, Peyton Manning, Serena Williams, or Abby Wambach. While stars such as these are the most visible professional athletes, they do not represent the majority. In fact, most of the athletes in their sports enjoy far less fame and fortune.

Professional athletes are also not limited to major US sports leagues. Athletes actually get paid to compete in just about any sport, from swimming to stock car racing. But even the top swimmers aren't guaranteed top salaries and product-endorsement deals.

There are many different sports and a variety of ways that

WHAT ATHLETES MAKE

Tiger Woods was the highest-paid athlete from June 2008 to June 2009, raking in $110 million.[1] The majority of that came from endorsement deals rather than prize money. No other athlete came close to matching Woods's earnings during that period. For comparison, NBA star Kobe Bryant made $45 million in the same time period. Kody Lostroh was the 2009 Professional Bull Riders World Champion, earning more than $1.6 million during the season. He had made between $273,000 and $298,000 in the three previous years.[2] Not all athletes pull in seven-figure or even six-figure salaries, however. Many of them need second jobs just to support themselves. In 2008, the Bureau of Labor Statistics reported that the average pro athlete made $79,460, meaning that many of them made far less than that.[3]

one can become a professional athlete. But it is important to remember that, while sports are fun, it is not easy to get to the professional level. The world is full of exceptional athletes who, for one reason or another, never had what it took to become a pro. As Boston Red Sox first baseman Kevin Youkilis said, "Your chances of becoming a professional athlete are not good."[4]

If you do decide to pursue a career as a professional athlete, be prepared to work hard and make some sacrifices. But for those who do make it to the top, get ready for an adventure.

WHAT IS A PROFESSIONAL ATHLETE'S WORK ENVIRONMENT?

The life of a professional athlete largely depends on what sport he or she is competing in and his or her level of success. A top National Football League (NFL) player might make a lot of money and be a big star. But an emerging track-and-field star might live at an Olympic Training Center with little notoriety and very little income. But when you cut out the money and the fame, professional athletes often have similar lifestyles.

Whether it be an NFL star or an unknown Olympic hopeful, a professional athlete's career demands a lot of time. Sports fans typically only see the games and competitions for a couple of hours on television. There is much more to being a professional athlete, however.

Many athletes have to live in different cities or on the road while competing. "[The hard part] is the daily grind and

Olympic stars such as Nastia Liukin spend years preparing in relative obscurity before competing on the biggest stage.

missing your family," said Boston Red Sox pitcher Jonathan Papelbon, who has a wife and two children. "We're playing 162 games a year, plus spring training and playoffs. Not being around your family is the hardest thing."[5] Even during the off-season, today's professional athletes are expected to work hard so that they are in top shape to start the next season.

Because of the physical nature of a sports career, athletes often experience injuries—some of them being very serious. Knowing that possibility, athletes realize the importance of doing their jobs correctly, in an effort to stay healthy. "If you worry about [getting hurt], then you're going to get banged up," Philadelphia Eagles coach Andy Reid said. ". . . If you're playing cautious football, then that's normally when injuries take place."[6]

The demands on a professional athlete are more than physical. Some elite athletes play in front of thousands of fans every day. Often, there will be millions more fans watching the games on television. With intense pressure from fans and media, the stress level for an athlete can soar. Prior to the 2010 Olympic Winter Games in Vancouver, British Columbia, US Alpine skier Lindsey Vonn was expected to be one of the brightest stars for Team USA, and she knew it. "In some ways, it is a lot of pressure," she said. "What's most important for me is just to stay focused on my own goals, and all I can do is do my best."[7] Although some people had unrealistic expectations for Vonn, she handled the pressure well. She won a gold medal and a bronze medal.

There are also some pitfalls of being a professional athlete. Many retired athletes—especially from high-contact sports such as football—experience chronic pains from the physical abuse their bodies took during their careers. Athletes also need to be careful about money. According to a report in *Sports Illustrated*, 78 percent of NFL players are

SELECT COMPANY

Even great athletes have a hard time getting jobs, simply because there are not a lot of opportunities. There were only about 16,500 professional athletes in the United States in 2008.[8] NFL teams have 53-man rosters, meaning that at any given time, there are only about 1,700 pro football players. MLB, NBA, and NHL teams have much smaller rosters, although in baseball and hockey, most athletes begin their careers in a minor league before being good enough to play at the top level.

either bankrupt or under financial stress within two years of retirement, and 60 percent of NBA players are broke within six years of retiring.[9] Professional athletes constantly have to be aware of bad business deals and other pressures, even from close friends and family.

HOW IS THE JOB MARKET FOR PROFESSIONAL ATHLETES?

When you think of a pro athlete, you probably think of a Major League Baseball (MLB) player, an NFL player, a National Hockey League (NHL) player, or an NBA player. But a career in professional athletics is not limited to these four major sports leagues. Even within those sports, there are hundreds of minor league athletes. Besides players in the big four US sports leagues, professional athletes are also race car drivers, boxers, soccer players, tennis players, swimmers, skiers, bull riders, and more. There are even professional leagues for popular sports such as lacrosse, motorcycle racing, and mixed martial arts.

Opportunities for women have increased in recent years, too. The Women's National Basketball Association (WNBA) began play in 1997. As of 2010, it had 12 teams competing in the league. Women's Professional Soccer began play in 2009 and had seven teams in 2010. There are also opportunities for women's softball players. After a hiatus, National Pro Fastpitch resumed play in 2004. That league had four teams in 2010.

No matter how you look at it, though, becoming a professional athlete is unlikely. There are only so many openings in the NBA, NFL, NHL, and MLB. The same goes for Olympic sports and emerging leagues such as Major League Soccer or the WNBA. But unlike stars in the major US leagues, many Olympic hopefuls and pro athletes competing in smaller sports cannot make a living solely through their sport and have to have second jobs. And no matter what the sport is, there will always be lots of competition for the few actual jobs as professional athletes.

A PROFILE OF A PROFESSIONAL ATHLETE

All-star infielder Kevin Youkilis has developed into one of the best players in the major leagues since his rookie year in 2004. He even helped the Boston Red Sox win a World Series championship. Although he has an incredible amount of natural talent, Youkilis has worked very hard to become the player he is today.

"It's a lot of work," he said. "You come to the field and prepare yourself as best as you can."[10] For Youkilis and many of his Red Sox teammates, that daily preparation includes a lot of film study, batting practice, and traveling. "It's a really repetitive day, and there's a lot of flying across the country all the time," Youkilis said. "There's not much excitement. You don't get to do much [outside of work] during the year."[11] The payoff can be tremendous, however. In addition to making millions of dollars, Youkilis has also won championships. But that's not even the best part, Youkilis said. "Just seeing the pride of your family and friends—how proud they are of you," he said. "That's probably the most rewarding thing.

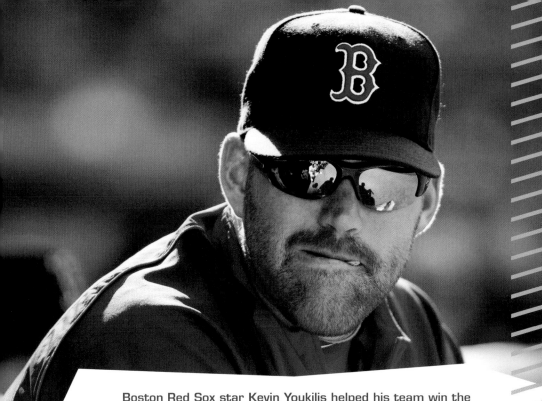

Boston Red Sox star Kevin Youkilis helped his team win the
2007 World Series title.

The World Series is great, and All-Star Games are really cool,
and everything is all enjoyable. But, when the closest people
to you really respect and love and care about what you do, it
means a lot."[12]

A DAY IN THE LIFE OF A
PROFESSIONAL ATHLETE

The fans see their favorite athletes for only a few hours at a
time when the athletes are competing. But athletes often arrive
at their stadiums or arenas several hours before game time to
prepare for that day's contest. When they aren't competing,
pro athletes spend long days practicing, doing strength
training, and preparing for competition in other ways.

Even if he or she isn't badly injured, a professional athlete often has little bumps and bruises from the intense training and competition. As such, one of the first stops an athlete makes on a given day is to the trainer's office. The trainer helps the athlete take care of his or her body. This is very important for professional athletes because they make their living based on their body's performance.

Perhaps more so than ever before, the daily routine of a professional athlete also includes study time. Athletes are constantly watching video of both their performance and of their opponents. Video can help an athlete identify a problem in his or her own technique. Likewise, video preparation can help a player or team prepare for what an opponent will do in an upcoming competition. Some athletes spend hours each day studying film.

Athletes also must spend countless

NOT YOUR AVERAGE CAREERS

When thinking of a professional athlete, most people would think of the major US sports that are covered on TV network ESPN. But there are dozens of other sports in which one can become a professional. The United States Olympic Committee sponsors more than 40 sports, ranging from gymnastics and figure skating to badminton and bobsledding. Action sports, such as skateboarding and snowboarding, are growing in popularity, too. Although they are still growing in the United States, sports such as rugby and cricket have popular leagues in other countries. Professional athletes even compete in running, surfing, roller skating, bowling, billiards, and darts.

Legendary quarterback Brett Favre returned for his twentieth NFL season in 2010.

hours practicing and improving their skills. What specifically an athlete does depends on the sport he or she is competing in. But a typical day almost always consists of stretching and warming up, actual practicing of the sport, and also weight lifting or some other form of physical conditioning.

These long days of training are all done in preparation for competition. When that day comes, an athlete will likely spend most of the day resting. Then, in the hours before the competition, an athlete visits the trainer to stretch and warm up. Afterward, the athlete talks to the press. Then he or she visits the trainer again after stretching and cooling down. For many athletes, competitions also mean travel, so much time is spent in hotels and on airplanes.

TOP FIVE QUESTIONS ABOUT BECOMING A PROFESSIONAL ATHLETE

1. *How do I know if I'm good enough to become a professional athlete?*

   It takes an elite athlete to be able to become a professional, and even then it's difficult. Typically, if you aren't already one of the best high school players in your state, your chances of becoming a professional are slim.

2. *Are there classes I should take to prepare myself for a career as an athlete?*

   For the most part, classes offered at a high school or collegiate level do not directly prepare student athletes to be professional athletes. However, there are certain classes that are beneficial for aspiring professional athletes. For example, it is a good idea to take business or finance classes. Since the playing career of a professional athlete is relatively short, and incomes can range from very high to very low, money management is very important. Other courses, such as physical education or nutrition, are helpful, too. It is very important that an athlete know how to take care of his or her body. Regardless of what the classes are, however, hopeful athletes are always advised to get a good education. Because the chances of making it as a professional athlete are so small—and the careers of most professional athletes are very short—having a career to fall back on is important.

3. *What training is required?*

    Regardless of what sport you are involved with, it is important to be in top physical condition. Weight training and cardiovascular work are essential for all athletes. Within each sport, there are specific workouts or training sessions needed to succeed.

4. *Do I need more than just great physical ability to make it as a professional athlete?*

    Yes, while talent and being in great physical condition are essential, they're not all an athlete needs. Every athlete experiences failure and will feel pressure to perform. Because of that, being strong mentally is just as important as being strong physically.

5. *How long do professional athlete careers last?*

    Although it varies by sport, injuries and age lead to relatively short careers in all sports. The average career for an NFL player is just 3.5 seasons[13], and for a MLB player, the average career lasts 5.6 years.[14] Other sports, such as auto racing and golf, can lead to longer careers.

Sisters Venus Williams, *right*, and Serena Williams won the
tennis doubles competition at the 2010 French Open.

WOULD YOU MAKE A GOOD PROFESSIONAL ATHLETE?

Not everyone has what it takes to become a
professional athlete. In fact, because it is so
difficult, Boston Red Sox star Kevin Youkilis said, "I wouldn't
recommend it as something for kids to look into as a career."[1]

However, Youkilis knows that, like him, many young people dream of becoming a professional athlete. There is nothing wrong with working hard and pursuing your dream. Sports offer many new opportunities and friendships, even if you never reach the top level. That is why Youkilis said young athletes should make sure they enjoy their sport more than anything else.

"As a high school kid, you just gotta' go have fun, practice and wherever it's going to take you, it's going to take you," Youkilis said. "There's no . . . way of doing it other than just having fun, enjoying it, and just getting better."[2]

LOVE FOR THE GAME

It's difficult to succeed at anything in life if you aren't passionate about it. Sports are the same way. If you want to be a pro baseball player, you better love standing in dirt while your opponent throws a five-ounce (0.14 kg) ball at you. If you want to be a pro bull rider, you should get a thrill out of climbing

HARD WORK PAYS OFF

Professional athletes often strive for one thing—to be the best. In order to get there, it takes a lot of hard work and determination. Tennis star Serena Williams had 13 Grand Slam singles titles to her credit as of 2010. "I hated the summers [while growing up]," she said. "We'd go [to practice] in the morning from 8 to 11 a.m. and then we have lunch at the park and right after that we'd go back to practice. It was tough. When you are that young you don't think about it. But it's those memories and all the hard work that you don't forget and eventually it pays off."[3]

on the back of a 2,000-pound (907-kg) bull that's mission is to throw you off. When Derek Jeter was a kid, he wanted nothing more than to play baseball for the New York Yankees. The 2010 season was his sixteenth as a Yankee. "Dreams become realities when you love what you're doing," he said.[4] Having a strong personal coach or mentor can be very helpful in making sure you stay on the right track for success.

PRACTICE MAKES PERFECT

Having athletic ability is essential. No athlete will make it as a professional without having incredible ability to perform on the playing field. If you're in good physical condition, you're off to a good start. From there, it simply takes practice—and lots of it—to make sure you have more ability and skill than others around you. This sometimes means sacrificing much of your social life

HAVE A BACKUP PLAN

In some sports, athletes have an opportunity to turn professional right after high school. Baseball is one of those sports. But Boston Red Sox pitcher Jonathan Papelbon played at Mississippi State University before beginning his professional baseball career. "My advice is to go to college," Papelbon said. "Those are the major years of developing. I've always felt like it's more important to go to college to try to figure out who you are and understand what life is about." In addition to maturing, Papelbon said he believes in a college education as insurance in case a career in pro sports doesn't work out. "If you don't make it as a player out of high school, life becomes a lot harder. If you don't make it as a player out of college, it doesn't become as hard," he said.[5]

After struggling early in his career, Landon Donovan, *left*,
refocused and helped Team USA win its group at the
2010 World Cup.

during high school and college. "Just work hard every single day," major league baseball player Marco Scutaro said. "The only way you can get better is working. It's a long process."[6]

STUDY YOUR SPORT

The skills required to succeed are different for each sport, so it is important to identify which skills you need for your sport and to be around people who can help you develop those skills. "I grew up going to the drag races to watch my dad," said drag racer Ashley Force. "All our family vacations were at the drag races. So I got to know all the other teams and the other drivers. When I was old enough to drive a street car, for my sixteenth birthday, I went to Frank Hawley's Drag Racing school and got my race license, and it kinda went from there."[7]

LONG ROAD AHEAD

The Cleveland Indians signed Marco Scutaro as an 18-year-old out of Venezuela in 1994. He didn't make it to the major leagues until eight years later, and even then it took another two years before he became a regular player in the majors. Scutaro and several other players are featured in the 2005 documentary *A Player To Be Named Later*, which shows the trials that minor league players go through in trying to make it big. "It's not easy, bro, I'm telling you," Scutaro said. "In the minors, you don't make no money and there's nothing. You're pretty much going out there and trying your best every single day without knowing if you're going to make it or not."[8]

CHECKLIST

Is a career as a professional athlete a good fit for you? Discover whether you've got what it takes with this checklist.

- *Do you have a passion for sports?*

- *Do you spend countless hours improving your skills in your favorite sport and keeping yourself in top physical condition?*

- *Are you mentally strong, and do you handle failure well?*

- *Are you focused and determined to succeed in the classroom as well as on the athletic field?*

- *Are you prepared to make sacrifices in terms of money or location in order to achieve your dream?*

If you answered yes to most of these questions, you are on the track to a career as a professional athlete. But even if you don't have a lot of these skills yet, you might still have a chance. Hard work and determination can go a long way toward helping you achieve your dream job.

HOW TO GET THERE

SET GOALS

If you have determined that you have what it takes to become a professional athlete, you will need to map out a plan on how to get to the professional ranks. Start by focusing on a target. If you're a football player, set a goal of one day competing in college and later in the NFL. If you're a tennis player, set a goal of winning Wimbledon or the US Open.

"I believe in setting goals really high," Jeter said. "Then, if you stumble, you still might be very good in the eyes of others. But, if you set them low, once you get there, you're going to be satisfied with what is probably not your best. You're never going to push yourself to achieve even more."[9]

MAKE A ROAD MAP FOR SUCCESS

Once you have a goal set, pinpoint the steps needed to achieve that goal. Regardless of your goal, the first step for any high school student should be a good education. "School is No. 1," Youkilis said. "You have to focus on that

SUCCESS IN SCHOOL EQUALS SUCCESS IN SPORTS

While going through school, you might wonder how your history or math classes are going to prepare you for a career as a professional athlete. There are great benefits to an education, however. An education can prepare you for a life after sports. But it can also make you a better player. The NFL Players Association (NFLPA) Web site said, "Players with [college] degrees earn 20 to 30 percent more than players who don't have degrees. They also have a career that lasts 50 percent longer."[10] The NFLPA said there isn't one reason for that but added that players with degrees show the "intelligence, concentration, and mental discipline" in school that can help them as players.[11] Of course, maintaining good grades also keeps you eligible to play for a college team.

number one because your chances of making it aren't that good. Even if you do make it, it's hard to stay up and have a career out of it. Some guys make it to the major leagues, but it doesn't mean you're going to make millions of dollars. That's not going to support you your whole life. The big thing is that at some point you're going to have to have another job. It's really important to get educated in a lot of different ways."[12]

PRACTICE, PRACTICE, PRACTICE

Off-the-field preparation is as important as anything for a hopeful professional athlete. Yet nothing can replace the importance of simply being the best at your sport, and the only way to do that is to work at it. Study your sport. Practice with your team. Practice with a private coach. Practice by yourself or with friends. Just practice. "For every pass I caught in a game, I caught a thousand passes in practice," said former football star Don Hutson, who is a member of the college football and pro football Halls of Fame.[13] While you might enjoy playing many sports, very few athletes ever compete in more than one

KEEP YOUR FOCUS

Reaching the ranks of a professional in your chosen sport requires a lot of dedication. It also demands that you strive for your goal every day. "In order to excel, you must be completely dedicated to your chosen sport," baseball Hall of Famer Willie Mays said. "You must also be prepared to work hard and be willing to accept constructive criticism. Without 100 percent dedication, you won't be able to do this."[14]

sport on the college level, much less at the pro level. That means that you might have to decide to specialize in one sport if you think you might have a shot to go pro in it.

IT'S NOT ALL SPORTS

Another important step off the field is developing high character and finding honest, trustworthy friends. When an athlete becomes famous, many people want to be affiliated with him or her. Some might offer business deals, others might offer opportunities to try new things. But not all of these are positive for an athlete's career or his or her position as a role model. "You have to worry about more stuff other than baseball, or whatever [sport] you do," Youkilis said. "You have to be a model citizen. You can't do anything stupid. You have to associate with the right crowd and not the wrong crowd. Hopefully you have a good family that can support you and point you in the right direction. There is so much stuff off the field that can ruin everything on the field."[15]

Cullen Jones, an Olympic gold medalist in swimming, spends his spare time working with a charity teaching kids how to swim.

Sports agents use their expertise in business and law to help athletes get the best jobs and contracts.

WHAT IS A
SPORTS AGENT?

In 1996, actor Tom Cruise played a sports agent in the film *Jerry Maguire.* The movie centered on the relationship between sports agent Jerry Maguire and his only client, football star Rod Tidwell, played by actor Cuba Gooding Jr.

Naturally, the story line was embellished a bit for Hollywood purposes. Maguire told Tidwell in the movie, "I will not rest until I have you holding a Coke, wearing your own shoe, playing a Sega game—featuring you—while singing your own song in a new commercial—starring you—broadcast during the Super Bowl, in a game that you are winning, and I will not sleep until that happens."[1] However, the general story was fairly accurate in depicting the role that an agent has in sports.

"I thought it was a little over-dramatized," sports agent Tom Mills said about his first impressions of the film. "But, I've seen it since the first time and they really did a pretty accurate portrayal on a lot of the conversations we have to have with our clients, a lot of the emotions the agent and player feel. The negotiations they went through, we experience those too."[2]

Just as in the movie, the life of a sports agent can be thrilling, emotional, fast paced, and rewarding. It's also a lot of work just to get into the field, and it can be a demanding job once you're there.

The role of an agent is, simply, to help athletes maximize their earning potential.

"SHOW ME THE MONEY!"

The 1996 film *Jerry Maguire* is an entertaining look at the world of a sports agent. The famous line in the film comes from football player Rod Tidwell, who tells his agent, "Show me the money!" HBO had a sitcom titled *Arli$$* that was about a sports agent and aired from 1996 to 2002.

Most notably, the agent negotiates the terms of an athlete's contract with a team—such as salary and length. Agents also find endorsement deals and negotiate those rates. "Really, it's just to represent [the players'] best interests in any capacity that they ask us to," said Mills, who is based in Boulder, Colorado. "We're all attorneys in our firm, and in that sense our duty is no different than any lawyer would have toward his or her legal client."[3]

WHAT IS A SPORTS AGENT'S WORK ENVIRONMENT?

There are thousands of sports agents. The Sports Agent Directory lists more than 3,500 sports agents from ten different sports leagues.[4] Mills said the NFL alone has roughly 800 certified agents listed in its directory.[5] With that type of competition, agents are in a constant push to gain—and retain—clients. That often requires nearly nonstop effort on the part of the agent. Sports agents can spend hours on the phone, text messaging, e-mailing, or faxing each day. They also spend a great deal of time traveling around the country.

KNOWLEDGE IS POWER

Representing a professional athlete can be exciting. However, it is important for an agent to know much more than just the sports in which his or her clients are involved. Agents need to know legal issues, be familiar with collective bargaining agreements in particular leagues, learn tax laws, and become well versed in business practices in general.

Agent Ron Shapiro, *left*, is known for helping star players get good deals with their current team. In 2010, his client Joe Mauer, *right*, re-signed with his hometown Minnesota Twins.

"I quickly learned that this was a 24–7 job in a personal services industry," said Jay Burton from International Management Group, one of the largest sports agencies in the world. "Sometimes the travel can be a real pain. As much as I love my job, I also enjoy having a personal life, but sometimes the two can conflict."[6]

HOW IS THE MARKET FOR A SPORTS AGENT?

In today's world, sport is a big-time business. Because of that, athletes in major professional leagues often demand high salaries and sign multimillion-dollar contracts. With so much at stake, Mills said, a player is better off letting someone else—the agent—handle negotiations. Mills works with NFL players, and the NFL has a set of rules that agents and teams must follow with contract negotiations.

"Each team has an expert on those rules whose entire job is to negotiate these contracts," Mills said. "If a player tried to [negotiate a contract] on his own, he would be at a very big experience and expertise disadvantage, compared to the team negotiator. If they make a bad error in negotiating on their own, they could leave a lot of money on the table. You want to make sure you have somebody on your side [who] knows the rules and can maximize your earning potential."[7]

A PROFILE OF A SPORTS AGENT

Mills became a sports agent in the mid-1990s, following in the footsteps of his father, Jack. Together, they represent past and present NFL players, ranging from Hall of Fame running back Eric Dickerson to former Denver Broncos great Rod Smith. They also represent many lesser-known or unknown players. Regardless of the status of the player, Mills keeps busy. During the NFL season, he spends a good portion of each day working with existing clients who are employed with NFL teams. Although contracts are already in place for those players, the players have medical needs and perhaps endorsements or personal appearances that the agent must arrange.

A DAY IN THE LIFE OF A SPORTS AGENT

The goal of a sports agent is to help his or her athlete clients become financially secure—not just during their playing career, but for life. To do that, an agent spends time negotiating top-dollar contracts and finding product-endorsement deals for star athletes. For lesser-known clients, the agent spends much of his or her time finding employment for the athlete.

A REWARDING CAREER

"I truly enjoy adding value to a player's career," said Jay Burton of the International Management Group. "Be it a small matter or an important achievement, such as delivering a significant multiyear endorsement contract, adding value to their life and career is what I like most about the job."[8]

Whether they are working with star athletes or not, agents must make sure they are keeping up with trends in the industry, and they must be certain they know the market in which their clients are involved. Because Mills works with NFL players, he spends part of every day keeping up with news on teams all throughout the league. For example, a player being cut by the Buffalo Bills could mean an opportunity for another player.

POTENTIAL FOR HIGH DOLLARS

Becoming a sports agent could be a lucrative career, but representing athletes in some sports does not bring instant wealth. Agents on average take approximately 3 or 4 percent of a client's salary.

So, with the minimum salary for an Arena Football Player being $28,000, an agent would only earn roughly $840 per year from some players.[10] However, agents who represent quality players in other leagues, such as the NBA, NFL, NHL, and MLB, can make a tremendous amount of money. The average salary for an MLB player is $2.8 million, which gives the agent an average of $84,000 per year for each of those players represented. In the NBA, an agent earns an average of $126,000 annually for the average $4.2 million player's salary. An NFL agent can earn $51,000 on the average $1.7 million player's salary, and an NHL agent can earn $54,000 on the average $1.8 million player's salary.[11]

In addition to negotiating contracts and endorsement deals, agents do a variety of other tasks, including offering advice on investments and taxes and providing financial counseling. A good chunk of the season is also spent working for the players who aren't employed. "Those guys want to keep playing," Mills said. "Our job for those guys is to try to get them back into the league with another team. You're looking at teams' injury needs after every Sunday. We're constantly evaluating those [injury] lists and contacting teams on behalf of our unemployed clients. That takes up a lot of our time in the season."[9]

Negotiation is an important aspect of being a sports agent.

While existing clients keep Mills busy during the season, prospective clients keep him busy all year. "We're almost always doing some form of new client development and recruiting," he said. "Whether it's summer or winter, there's always something going on in client development."[12]

TOP FIVE QUESTIONS ABOUT BECOMING A SPORTS AGENT

1. *How do I know whether I have the skills to become a sports agent?*

    Being a sports agent demands a lot. Common attributes of a successful sports agent include intelligence, a strong work ethic, sharp research skills, good organization, and being a strong negotiator. It is also important to have good people skills, which help when finding new clients and to keep existing ones comfortable.

2. *What can I do to prepare for a career as a sports agent?*

    Getting an education is perhaps the most important requirement. Because sports agents are in such a competitive market, it is advised that those who want to join the field get an advanced degree, such as a master's degree in business or a law degree. Networking is also important. By volunteering or interning with an agency, you can get experience and showcase yourself to the people there. If you do a good job, it could help your chances of being hired. One common phrase is "It's not who you know, it's who knows you."

3. *To be a successful sports agent, is it important to love sports?*

    Not necessarily. In fact, because of the nature of the job, it is more important to have a passion for business or law than it is to love sports.

4. *Are there advancement opportunities for agents?*

    Yes, many who are just beginning in the business will get started as apprentices in large sports marketing firms. From there, they can advance to become agents and then, down the road, executives at firms.

5. *How much money do sports agents make?*

    Because an agent's salary is largely dependent on commission, that answer depends on the clients the agent represents. The better the client performs on the field or court, the more earning potential the agent has. It is not uncommon for top agents to make more than $1 million annually. However, the average salary for a sports agent is just over $58,000, according to payscale.com.[13]

5

Agent Scott Boras, *right*, helped baseball player Adrian Beltre sign with the Boston Red Sox in 2007.

WOULD YOU MAKE A GOOD SPORTS AGENT?

Being a sports agent can be an exciting and rewarding career, but it can also be taxing. It's important to make sure you know what you're getting into when you pursue a career as a sports agent. If you're interested in the business side of sports, this could be a great fit. But if you're simply a fan looking to be involved with the athletes, working as a sports agent might not be the best choice.

"If you stay the course, get a little luck and good timing to come your way, and, most of all, put in a lot of hard work, it can lead to a rewarding financial career path," said Jay Burton, a sports agent with International Management Group.[1]

NOT NECESSARILY SPORTS FANS

In a lot of sports careers, it stands to reason that having an interest in sports would be important. For a sports agent, however, enjoying sports isn't necessarily a requirement. In fact, having an interest in business or a focus on law is more important. "I would agree with that," said agent Mills. "We certainly watch our share of football in this office, but we don't really watch it the way the typical

SIGN OF THE TIMES

Years ago, sports agents spent a good deal of their time talking on the phone with clients and potential clients. The job still requires a lot of time on the phone, but not as much as in the past. Social networking is wildly popular among high school students. Sports agents are also putting it into play. "Kids [who] are currently in college, they're used to [social networking] and they like to text," agent Mills said. "It's much easier to communicate with them via that form than it would be to try to get them on the phone."[2]

Agent Drew Rosenhaus addressed the media while one of his clients, NFL star Terrell Owens, looked on after Owens was suspended in 2005.

fan does anymore. We almost look at it as a businessman would."[3]

If you're interested in becoming a sports agent, make sure you are well rounded. A background in business, law, or accounting is important.[4] Having an interest in sports will help, too, as you will need to stay current on what is happening in your clients' particular sport.

COMMUNICATION IS KEY

Once you've developed an interest in one, or all, of those areas, it is important to sharpen your skills in the areas that will make you a successful agent for a player. No skill is more important to an agent than the ability to negotiate. To become a good negotiator and maximize your clients' earning potential, your personality will play a role in your career. Because of that, you will need to learn to develop relationships and communicate well.[5]

KNOWING YOUR STUFF

Another key to successful negotiating is proper research. "You have to learn what's fair competition for your client, and that requires you researching the contracts around the league and what players are making," Mills said. "When it comes to negotiations, preparation is critical. Before you get started in [a negotiation], you really have to know your players, you have to know his strengths and weaknesses, you have to know the

IN THE NEWS

Several sports agents have become celebrities in their own right. Super agents, such as Scott Boras, Drew Rosenhaus, and Leigh Steinberg, have mega-stars on their client list. Often, the media goes through the agent to find out about contract negotiations with a player. Because they represent the players, the agents get quoted and become well known among sports fans. Therefore, it is important for aspiring sports agents to learn how to communicate with the media in a professional manner.

clubs you are negotiating with, and I think it helps to know the negotiator a little bit so you know their style."[6]

It is also important to know each state's laws about contacting amateur athletes, particularly those in college. Improper contact from an agent can take away an amateur athlete's eligibility and handicap a team. In 2010, the University of Southern California football team had to give up its 2005 national championship retroactively because a former player had received improper benefits from a potential agent. The team also lost scholarships and received a two-year ban from the postseason due to the charge.

CHECKLIST

Is being a sports agent right for you? Take a look at the checklist to see whether this career is a good fit.

- *Do you have an interest in business, law, or accounting?*

- *Do you enjoy following sports?*

- *Do you have good communication skills and develop good relationships with people?*

- *Are you good at doing research?*

- *Are you willing to put in extra hours to satisfy your client?*

If most of your answers were yes, a sports agent could be the career for you. If you answered no to many of the questions, you can still follow this path. If you work hard and expand your interests, anything is possible.

HOW TO GET THERE

FIND BUSINESS EXPERIENCE

Once you have determined that you have an interest in becoming a sports agent, you need to develop a career path. That begins in the classroom while you're in high school. Although most high school classes are similar for all students, there are certain courses you can take, and extracurricular activities in which you can be involved, that will jump-start your experience.

Any kind of business knowledge or familiarity you can get at a young age will help you in the long run. Joining the Future Business Leaders of America or getting involved with Junior Achievement in high school is a great way for you to get started in business. "Anything that will give you good experience and a work ethic, and if you're fortunate to get entry-level work at a company in the field of sports, all the better," Mills said.[7]

GETTING STARTED

One good way to get a feel for a career as a sports agent is to become involved with an internship, most likely while in college. Through an internship, you can get a glimpse of different areas of the field. It might be easiest for you to secure an internship through a smaller firm or with an individual agent. International Management Group, one of the largest sports agency firms in the world, also has internship possibilities, but not many. It receives roughly 1,000 intern applications a year, with only 70 being accepted.[8]

Education is very important for an aspiring agent. Many agents have advanced law or business degrees.

STUDY HARD

No matter what classes you take in high school, make sure you produce good grades. "You need to get good enough grades to get to college and ultimately complete college and get to grad school," Mills said.[9] Following high school graduation, plan to major in a field that will prepare you for a career as a sports agent—such as business, accounting, or pre-law. Because sports management is such a competitive field, it is recommended to obtain a graduate degree as well. In addition to academic studies, you will want to pursue an internship in business or sports management.

GET CERTIFIED, THEN GET CLIENTS

Finally, in some cases, you need to pass a certification test. Most professional leagues require certification before you can begin working as an agent.

Of course, that's all the easy part of the job. Once you're certified, you've still got to get clients. "The hard part once you're certified is getting clients," Mills said. "That's the biggest challenge you face is recruiting new prospects. That's probably the biggest barrier to entry."[10]

FINDING CLIENTS

As you look ahead to a career as a sports agent, you'll surely see super agents, such as Scott Boras and Leigh Steinberg, representing their famous baseball and football clients. But don't focus solely on the major professional sports. Professional sports have numerous opportunities for athletes, which means numerous prospective clients for agents. Although competition for those clients will be fierce, don't forget about the soccer players, rodeo cowboys, swimmers, and track-and-field athletes who need representation as well. Also remember that professional sports opportunities for women have expanded in recent years, so the potential for representing female athletes is greater than ever before.

When he retired in 1997, Grambling State football coach
Eddie Robinson's 408 wins were the most of any college football
coach. He spent 55 seasons there.

WHAT IS A COLLEGE COACH?

C oaches play an important role on any team. They
teach, they motivate, and they keep the team
organized. It is their job not only to guide the team to
success, but also to help the athletes reach their full potential.

In college athletics, coaches also play a significant role in the lives of their players. Not only do they teach and motivate the players, they also serve as mentors at a key developmental time in a young person's life. "That's what I do now: I lead and I teach," said Duke University men's basketball coach Mike Krzyzewski. "If we win basketball games from doing that, then that's great, but I lead and teach. Those are the two things I concentrate on."[1]

WHAT IS A COLLEGE COACH'S WORK ENVIRONMENT?

Working as a college coach is not for the person who wants to sit at a desk all day. In fact, there will be very little time spent in front of a desk. Depending on the sport you choose to coach, you will be working outside a lot, sometimes in bad weather, or inside a gymnasium. Travel is also likely involved, and, depending on the school at which you are employed, it could be by bus, train, or airplane.

The majority of college coaches are assistants and may have rigorous schedules only during the season. Life for a

WHAT COACHES MAKE

While there is potential to make a lot of money in college coaching, the majority of coaches do not. In 2008, the median earnings were $39,550, according to the US Department of Labor. The lowest 10 percent of all coaches made less than $15,530.[2] The high-profile coaches make much more. In 2009, University of Southern California football coach Pete Carroll made $4.4 million.[3]

head coach can often be rigorous throughout the whole year. College coaches constantly have to think about recruiting. In sports such as football and basketball, the coaches are often high-profile members of the community and are expected to maintain a public presence.

"The only off-season that a college [basketball] coach has is the last two weeks in May and the first two weeks in August. That's it," said Barry Hinson, the former men's basketball coach at Oral Roberts and Missouri State.[4]

That can be especially hard on a coach's family. "A family, no question, will struggle with college coaching," said Hinson, who has a wife and two daughters. "There's peaks and valleys. You're never home. You're always on the road recruiting. You're either at practice, you're at the gym, you're at the office.

KEEPING UP WITH TECHNOLOGY

Coaching college athletics is not what it used to be. Neither is recruiting college athletes. Using Facebook, Twitter, and text messaging are now regular tasks for college coaches. "Coaching has changed dramatically in 30 years, more so than anything because of social media," said former Missouri State men's basketball coach Barry Hinson. "It has changed our sport dramatically. In this day and age, you've got to be tech-savvy."[5] Because high school and college-aged youth are so involved with online social networking, coaches find it easier to communicate with potential recruits and their own athletes using those media. Coaches also must be aware of the rules, as the NCAA frequently updates its rules about contact using social media.

You have to have a strong [partner]. I've been fortunate, but it's hard on family." [6]

Another challenging aspect of college coaching is the stress involved. With so much money invested into college athletics—especially football and basketball—there is a lot of pressure on the coaches to succeed. A coach's job security is often directly tied to his or her win-loss record. While at Missouri State, Hinson had a very successful team. But his team always managed to come up just a little short of advancing to the National Collegiate Athletic Association (NCAA) Tournament, and Hinson eventually lost his job. "No question, there's pressure," he said. "You've got to make it to the Tournament." [7]

Some coaches also face pressure from outside sources, such as the press. Programs such as the Duke men's basketball team, the Notre Dame football team, or the Connecticut women's basketball team are constantly in the news. Their fans expect the team to win championships, and the media fishes for every story involved with the program. "[At Kansas] whatever you say, whether it be in print, whether it be an interview on the radio, you're under a microscope," said Hinson, who is now the director of men's basketball at the University of Kansas. "There is an article in the paper about KU basketball every day." [8]

HOW IS THE JOB MARKET FOR A COLLEGE COACH?

If you have considered a career in coaching and have a passion for teaching, there are numerous opportunities at all levels of college athletics. Hundreds of colleges field sports teams in one of the NCAA's three divisions. Collegiate teams compete in sports from football to gymnastics to skiing. Most of those teams also have assistants in addition to a head coach.

SET A GOAL, AND GO FOR IT

"When you are passionate, you always have your destination in sight, and you are not distracted by obstacles," said Krzyzewski. "Because you love what you are pursuing, things like rejection and setbacks will not hinder you in your pursuit. You believe that nothing can stop you!"[13]

In 2008, there were approximately 225,000 coaches and scouts employed in the United States. The Bureau of Labor Statistics projects that number to increase to more than 281,000 by 2018.[9] Of course, that number includes scouts as well as youth, high school, and professional coaches, all in addition to college coaches. But, college coaches do make up a significant percentage of that 225,000.

University of Colorado sports teams compete in Division I, which is the highest level of college sports. Colorado's athletic department alone employs nearly 60 coaches.[10] At Garden City Community College in Kansas, there are more than 25 coaches on staff.[11] Considering there are more than 7,000 colleges in the United States, many of which offer athletics, there are thousands of coaches in the collegiate ranks today.[12]

Scouts are becoming increasingly important in college sports.

A PROFILE OF A COLLEGE COACH

Hinson has been involved with coaching for nearly 30 years, with more than half of that time spent in college coaching. He began as a high school coach, though, working first as an assistant and then eight years as a head coach. After that, he served as an assistant coach at Oral Roberts for four years, at which point he was named the head coach. After two winning seasons, he became the head coach at Missouri State. Throughout his career, Hinson has been a head coach in college basketball for 11 seasons, producing a winning record in ten of them. He is the fourth-winningest coach in Missouri State basketball history. In 2010, Hinson was named the director of men's basketball operations at the University of Kansas. It is not uncommon for coaches to move into other administrative or leadership roles within a program when they finish coaching.

A DAY IN THE LIFE OF A COLLEGE COACH

Depending on the size of the school and the sport, coaches will all have slightly different routines. At smaller schools, such as those in Division III, some coaches also work as professors at the university. Coaches in high-profile sports at big, Division I schools usually dedicate themselves solely to coaching their team. Hinson points to the coach of the Kansas men's basketball team, Bill Self, as an example of what a high-profile college coach might experience on a given day.

University of Kansas men's basketball coach Bill Self guided his team to the NCAA championship in 2008.

University of Tennessee women's basketball coach Pat Summitt is one of the most successful college coaches in any sport.

During the season, Hinson said, a typical day for coach Self will begin around 9:00 a.m. "I would say the first two hours of his morning [are] going to be doing stuff through appointments through his administrative assistant—phone interviews, TV interviews, print interviews, answering phone calls, answering e-mails," Hinson said. A staff meeting, a business lunch, and a practice planning session usually follow. Then, after all that, the team goes through practice. Following practice, Self goes back to his office for "recruiting calls, more interviews, watching game film, or recruiting videos," Hinson said. The day will often end at around 10:00 or 11:00 p.m. "Next day, it starts all over again," Hinson said.[14]

> ## ANOTHER OPTION
>
> If you're not sure whether coaching is for you, you may consider a related career by getting into sports administration. High schools and colleges have athletic directors who coordinate all the athletic programs at their schools. They take care of budgets, scheduling games, and other administrative duties.

For Self and the rest of the Kansas staff, the off-season is busy, too. Although the schedule is different, the days are still long, as the staff goes through camps, spends countless hours traveling the country to recruit players, and watches game films. For a high-profile coach such as Self, meeting with the press is often a year-round duty as well.

TOP FIVE QUESTIONS ABOUT BECOMING A COLLEGE COACH

1. *How do I know whether I have the skills to become a college coach?*

   Being a college coach requires you to have a high volume of knowledge about the sport you want to coach. You also need to display leadership qualities and be comfortable as a public speaker.

2. *What classes could I take in high school to prepare for coaching?*

   Any type of exercise classes or classes dealing with the human body would be helpful to any prospective coach. Communications classes also could be beneficial, such as a public speaking class. An overall education is very important for prospective coaches, however.

   In order to teach or coach at the high school level, the person will most likely need a teaching certificate. Many college coaches also have master's degrees.

3. *Is it important to be a good athlete before becoming a coach?*

   Not necessarily. Being an athlete will certainly help you obtain a knowledge of the sport you want to coach. However, many successful coaches were never high-level players in the sport they coach. If you can't play for your high school team, volunteer to help the team in any possible way.

4. *How much job security do college coaches have?*

Not much. In college, winning is important. If you're a winning coach, your chances of keeping your job—or even improving your job status—are good. If you don't win, your job could be short-lived. A large number of college coaches get fired at some point in their careers. However, some coaches enjoy long careers. University of Tennessee women's basketball coach Pat Summitt has held her job since 1974. John Gagliardi, the football coach at Division III St. John's University in Minnesota, has been at the helm since 1953. He is the winningest coach in NCAA history.

5. *Are there opportunities for women to coach in college athletics?*

Definitely. Women's athletics have expanded at the college level, and hundreds of colleges around the country have women's coaching positions available in a variety of sports, such as basketball, volleyball, softball, track and field, golf, gymnastics, and more.

UCLA softball coach Kelly Inouye-Perez, *right*, congratulated one of her players during the 2010 Women's College World Series.

WOULD YOU MAKE A GOOD COLLEGE COACH?

A college coach must be not only a fan of the sport he or she is coaching but also a disciplined, dedicated, and natural leader.

PASSION FOR THE GAME

A coach needs to have knowledge and a passion for the sport he or she is coaching. Coaches also need to have a passion for teaching and leading, because that, in essence, is the root of coaching athletics. "I don't look at myself as a basketball coach. I look at myself as a leader who happens to coach basketball," Duke coach Krzyzewski said.[1]

Although the highest-profile coaches are famous and make a lot of money, most young coaches live in relative obscurity and make little money. Without a deep passion for the game and for coaching, it is a hard profession to survive in.

"I would recommend it for the person that gets it," said Hinson. "If you're getting into college coaching for aesthetic reasons, you're going to be really disappointed. If you're getting into college coaching for the right reasons, it could be the most rewarding thing you've ever seen."[3]

LASTING IMPACT

While coaching can be a stressful profession, it can also be very rewarding. College coaches get to spend their lives helping young, driven men and women achieve their goals. "You . . . get to stay young," Hinson said. "You get a chance to be around kids every day, and you get an opportunity to have an impact in somebody's life."[2]

COACHES COMMUNICATE

After determining you have the desire to get into coaching, it's important to identify the skills that will make you a

HOW TO GET INVOLVED

There are several ways for you to get involved with a team. While in high school, talk to a coach in your school, and ask him or her about how you can help the team—as either a team manager or a student assistant. There are also opportunities for high school students to get involved with coaching youth on a voluntary basis. Contact your local YMCA or youth organizations, and ask how you can help.

successful college coach. Hinson believes that good coaches have to be good communicators. "No question, you've got to be able to communicate with people," he said.[4] Communication is key because coaches have to work with their players and assistant coaches as well as speak to the community and media. Organization, leadership, and management skills are also essential.

COPING WITH STRESS

Another key element to being a successful coach is an ability to handle stress. College coaches are under intense pressure to win games and to keep their athletes in line academically so they can graduate. Coaches at all levels of athletics deal with stress on some level. "You have to have thick skin, and you've got to be resilient," Hinson said. "If you're not, then you don't need to do it."[5]

CHECKLIST

Is a career as a college coach a good fit for you? Discover whether you've got what it takes with this checklist.

- *Do you have an interest in sports?*

- *Do you have a desire to teach?*

- *Do you have good communication skills?*

- *Are you able to handle stress well?*

- *Have you shown an ability to work well with others?*

- *Do you have a passion to lead?*

If you answered yes to most of these questions, a career as a college coach might be the right fit for you. If you answered no to most of them, there are many other jobs within college sports that might be a better fit for you.

HOW TO GET THERE

TAKE SOME CLASSES

As you are choosing classes to take during high school, or even college, find classes that may help you develop the skills you need to be a coach. Participating in sports is one of the best steps you can take toward learning the fundamentals you will one day teach. In addition, take fitness classes or even biology classes so you can learn about the human body and how to treat it. Any class that will develop your communication skills, such as English or speech, will help you as well. Because social media and technology have become such a big part of the coaching profession, courses that develop skills in those areas would be beneficial for any potential coach as well.

TEACHING SKILLS FOR LIFE

Every coach has to know the fundamentals of his or her sport and how to teach them to the players. But great coaches can't simply rely on the x's and o's of the game. Some of the best coaches learn how to cultivate relationships with their players, which helps them better motivate the athletes.

John Wooden is renowned for coaching the UCLA men's basketball team to a 620–147 record and an unprecedented 10 national championships during his 27 years there. He was also known for teaching his athletes life skills. "Coach Wooden enjoyed winning, but he did not put winning above everything," former player Kareem Abdul-Jabbar said. "He was more concerned that we became successful as human beings, that we earned our degrees, that we learned to make the right choices as adults and as parents."[6]

STAY IN SCHOOL

Colleges are great places for aspiring coaches to get started. In fact, many coaches get their start as volunteers or graduate assistants for an athletic program at their own college. However, it is also important to do well in the classroom in general. "The best thing is just to get a degree," Hinson said. "If you don't have a degree, you've got no shot."[7] Although most schools do not offer a degree in coaching, a bachelor's degree is required for many college coaches.

CLIMB THE LADDER

Once you have your degree, you will most likely have to start working your way up the coaching ladder. You probably won't start your coaching career by getting hired as a head coach at the university of your choice. Many college coaches begin their careers with jobs coaching high school teams or other youth sports clubs.

STUDY, STUDY, STUDY

There is no better way to learn the fundamentals of sport than by studying up on them. Being involved with a sport is one way to do that, but it's not the only way. Local libraries have a plethora of books that teach athletes the skills required to be successful in sports. If you want to become a coach, read those books and absorb any knowledge you can so that you can one day pass that on to your players.

Sherri Coale, the coach for the University of Oklahoma women's basketball team, began her coaching career as an assistant high school coach. Then she served as the head coach at Norman High School in Oklahoma for seven years before being hired at the University of Oklahoma.[8]

NETWORK

As with most professions, one of the best ways to reach the top is through networking. Head coaches often hire assistants they already know. Even if you don't play a sport in college, get to know the coaches, and do what you can to help them. "My greatest advice to kids, and I tell them this every day, is find a way to get connected to a person and to a program," Hinson said.[9] Identify particular colleges at which you would like to one day be a coach, and then get to know the people associated with those schools.

When Hinson began his career as a basketball coach, he started at the junior high level and then worked his way up to the lower levels of high school. Finally, at the age of 26, he became a head coach at a high school in Tulsa, Oklahoma. Throughout that time, he took his teams to camps at area colleges. At those camps, he got to know the college coaches. It was those people who eventually helped him get into college coaching. At Oral Roberts, Hinson first worked as an assistant under coach Bill Self. The two now work together again at the University of Kansas.

Specialty coaches, such as strength coaches, are common among college teams.

Sports fans rely on the information obtained and passed along by sports journalists, so it is important that the journalists get as much information as possible.

WHAT IS A
SPORTSWRITER?

The definition of a sportswriter is changing every day. Many years ago, a sportswriter was somebody who followed a team or an athlete and wrote about what the team or athlete did, usually for a newspaper or magazine.

Since most sports were not televised until recently, the fans relied on the journalists to know what was going on.

As technology has changed, however, so has journalism. Soon print journalists were working alongside reporters from television stations and eventually from Web sites. As television and then the Internet gave fans great—and instant—access to their teams, the role of the sportswriter has changed, too. The reporters now need to do much more than just write about what happened. They are now expected to write more human-interest features about the athletes, to delve deeper into issues, and sometimes to analyze.

CHANGING WORLD

Several years ago, sports journalists had three ways to connect with the public—through newspapers or magazines, on television, or on the radio. Today, there are a variety of forms of sports journalism. In addition to the traditional formats, sports journalists have had to become familiar with using Facebook, Twitter, blogs, online chats, podcasts, and other multimedia formats.

WHAT IS A SPORTSWRITER'S WORKING ENVIRONMENT?

Fans rely on sports journalists to report objectively on the goings-on of a team. After all, journalists have more access to the players, coaches, and executives than the fans have. But not all sports journalists have the same duties. Two of the most common types of sportswriters, however, are the beat reporters and the sports columnists.

A beat writer is assigned to cover a certain team, or beat. If you are a beat reporter for the Green Bay Packers, for example, it is your job to stay on top of everything going on with the team. So, you might write about their game on Sunday, a free agent signing on Monday, and a coaching change on Tuesday. Beat writers attend practices and games to make sure they always have the most up-to-date information. Depending on the team and the employer, beat writers often travel to away games, too.

A sports columnist is typically not assigned to cover one particular team. Rather, he or she covers the biggest story of the day while also offering an opinion. A sports columnist in Chicago might write opinions about the Chicago Bears, Chicago White Sox, and Chicago Fire in a single week. However, each of those teams would have their own beat writer to cover them on a daily basis. Because columnists have the freedom

BEHIND THE SCENES

The best-known sports journalism jobs are those of a sportswriter or sports broadcaster. However, if you love sports, but you're not interested in writing or being in front of a camera or microphone, there are still opportunities for you. Newspapers have sports page designers and copy editors. Although they don't often get to attend games, they can still be involved with sports. Newspapers also have sports photographers who go to the games and take photos for use online and in print. Radio and television stations have positions for producers and cameramen. In some of those jobs, you will have an opportunity to attend games and talk to players and coaches.

to express personal opinions, and their columns are often marked with their picture, they are often the best-known writers at a given media outlet.

Beat writers and sports columnists can work for newspapers, magazines, or Web sites. There are other types of sports journalists, however. These include sports broadcasters and editors.

Being a sportswriter can be very exciting, and it is often a career that others will envy. After all, sportswriters get free passes to sporting events, which allow them to sit in the press box and even go to the locker room and talk to the athletes.

However, the job comes with challenges. The typical sportswriter will not become wealthy. For many sportswriters just starting their careers, a salary in the low $20,000-per-year range is typical. Many never make much more than $40,000 in a year.[1] For some higher-profile sports journalism jobs—such as major sports columnists and broadcasters—the salary can top $100,000 per year, but those opportunities are not common.

Another challenge can be the schedule. A beat writer who covers an MLB team, for example, could be on the road for a large chunk of the season—including most of the spring, while the team trains in either Florida or Arizona. Following spring training is a 162-game schedule, half of which is played on the road. With so many games now starting in the evening, sportswriters often have to work late into the night. Sports contests often take place on weekends or holidays such as Thanksgiving or Christmas, too.

Sportswriters often use recorders while interviewing to ensure they are accurate in their reporting.

Sportswriters also have to work on deadlines. Depending on when a given game ends, sometimes a writer will have as little as 20 minutes to write an entire story. With the Internet, readers demand information instantly. That means pressure for the writer to produce a story as quickly as possible. Magazine writers usually have more time, but their work is usually longer and more in-depth.

HOW IS THE JOB MARKET FOR SPORTSWRITERS?

Although demand for sports news continues to rise, the market for sportswriters is weak. The news industry in general has struggled in the first decade of the twenty-first century. Almost all news organizations have cut staff to save money. Some prominent newspapers, such as the *Rocky Mountain News* in Denver and the *Seattle Post-Intelligencer*, have shut down after more than 100 years of operation.[2] From July of 1990 to July of 2009, the number of jobs in newspapers declined from more than 450,000 to around 275,000.[3]

There are still opportunities for aspiring sportswriters. Although many newspapers are struggling, most cities have some newspaper that covers sports. Some Web sites have also emerged into major sources for sports news, such as

EXPANDING YOUR KNOWLEDGE

Over the past couple of decades, sports journalism has gone well beyond the field. Reports of athletes getting into legal trouble are a part of the sports news every day. Contract negotiations and labor disputes are also a large part of the sports news landscape. "At some point, you need to be familiar with the world outside of sports if you're going to cover sports," said Jayson Stark of ESPN.com. "I've covered labor [issues], I've learned more medical school terminology than I ever thought I'd learn. If you're going to cover sports in modern-day America, you need to know a lot more than just how many balls in a walk and how many strikes in a strikeout and how many outs in an inning."[4]

Having a passion for writing is a good starting point for any aspiring sportswriter.

ESPN.com and Yahoo! Sports. As traditional print media has struggled, many professional teams and leagues have also begun hiring journalists to work directly for the teams' Web sites. However, you should be aware that many smaller online news sources, including most blogs, are done on a voluntary basis. Since many of these sites do not have a history of producing fair and objective journalism, their writers are not always granted the same team access as writers from newspapers and more established Web sites.

A PROFILE OF A SPORTSWRITER

Jayson Stark is one of the most respected baseball writers in the United States. He became a senior writer for ESPN.com in 2000 and covers MLB. He has built his reputation as a fair and reliable journalist during a career that has lasted more than 30 years. Before joining ESPN.com, he spent 21 years at the *Philadelphia Inquirer*.

"It's a great career," he said. "There just aren't as many jobs as there ought to be. That's the tough part. I'm doing exactly what I always dreamed of doing all my life, except I didn't know the Internet was going to exist."[5]

In addition to all of his writing and research for ESPN.com, Stark is constantly on the radio and TV, as well as attending games around the country.

BREAKING NEWS

"The biggest thing that hammered me over the head when I got to ESPN and ESPN.com is what a 24/7 world it was and is," Stark said. "It's not a tomorrow-morning world anymore. It's a right-now world. Most of the time I was in newspapers, reporting and breaking stories was a huge deal. But if I got a story at 3 o'clock in the afternoon, my job involved basically trying to sit on that story all day and all night [until the next morning], protecting that story and hoping nobody else knew, praying nobody else knew, doing whatever I could to make sure nobody else knew. Now, everybody is looking not just to break stories, but to break them 30 seconds before somebody else. It's really created a completely different work environment, not just for me and for people in the media, but for the people we cover."[6]

A DAY IN THE LIFE OF A SPORTSWRITER

For Stark and many other journalists, the days can be long and tiresome. Whether you are a beat writer, a columnist, or a broadcaster, preparation is needed before you even get to the game you are covering. Even if you are covering a high school football game, you need to know about the competing teams—their win-loss records, key players, and, if possible, their tendencies on the field.

As such, Stark's days are consumed by baseball. Since he covers the sport nationally, he makes sure he is on top of what's going on with all 30 MLB teams. He often wakes up early in the morning to watch video and read up on everything that happened in baseball the night before. He keeps track of the sports with three stat books, including:

> How every team is doing, whether they're hot, whether they're cold, whether they score runs or don't score runs. How the pitching is faring. I do all of that, because when you have to cover 30 teams, anything I can do to make sure I pay attention to every team is worth doing. I don't ever want to feel that a day gets by me, that games get by me. [7]

During the games, sportswriters often take stats, write notes, and maybe even work on writing their stories while using a laptop. When the game is over, the real work begins. After the games, the reporters typically go to the locker room to gather quotes from players and coaches. Then they head back to their computers, where they often have to write as least one story on deadline.

Sports reporters must be able to take diligent notes so they can accurately pass information along to their readers.

TOP FIVE QUESTIONS ABOUT BECOMING A SPORTSWRITER

1. *How do I know whether I've got the skills to become a sportswriter?*

   If you've already got a passion for writing, along with a passion for sports, you're off to a good start.

2. *Are there advancement opportunities in sports journalism?*

   Although it is a tough market to enter, there are opportunities to move up. Many sports journalists start off at smaller newspapers or radio or TV stations. If you excel at what you do and network with others in your industry, there could be opportunities to move up.

3. *How much do I need to know about the game in order to succeed?*

   Fans who follow your work are looking to you as an expert, so it is important to know what you're talking about. As you are working to get into a sports journalism career, however, you can't focus on an individual sport. It would help you to know as much as you can about a variety of sports. In fact, many young journalists begin by covering high school or small college sports before they start writing about the big college and professional sports.

4. *Can I really get into big games for free and meet the players?*

   If you are fortunate enough to get to a point where you are covering big-time college and professional athletics, you will be able to get press passes to events such as the World Series and Super Bowl. And you can't cover those events without talking to the players. However, it is stressed that journalists should not be fans of the players and teams they are covering. A journalist is expected to provide objective reporting, no matter what.

5. *How much education do I need to get started?*

   As with a lot of careers, it is highly recommended that you obtain an undergraduate degree in some field of study. For some sports journalism jobs, a graduate degree may be required, too. Many colleges offer journalism degrees, and many journalists get their start at their high school and college newspapers.

Sports journalism can be a very hectic, competitive field as reporters work to stay up-to-date and to break stories.

WOULD YOU MAKE A GOOD SPORTSWRITER?

I f you have a desire to get into sports journalism, it is most likely because you have an interest in sports. That is a good place to start, because the more you enjoy sports, the more you can pour your heart and soul into your career.

WOULD YOU MAKE A GOOD SPORTSWRITER?

Simply enjoying sports will not cut it, however. You must develop a variety of skills, including being able to write, interview, and communicate in an eloquent way. If you are in high school, do you enjoy classes that require writing assignments? If you do, that could indicate this is a career for you. Sportswriter Jonathan Rand discovered his talent for writing after seeing how well he did on an essay in high school. He eventually learned to combine that talent with his love for sports. "I decided the two things I liked best were sports and writing," he said. "So I figured it would be great if I could combine the two for a career."[1]

> ## LESS THAN GLAMOROUS
>
> No doubt, the thought of going to the Super Bowl, NBA Finals, or Olympic Games has inspired you to consider a career in sports journalism. However, many in the field begin at a much lower level. Chances are that if you want to become a sportswriter, you will begin your career at a small newspaper in a town you've never heard of. And, instead of covering big-time events, you will be asked to write a story about a Little League baseball player. Or you will be assigned to answer phones and e-mails and do other tasks that never get attention.[2] These are all building blocks in the foundation of becoming a good journalist, though.

THE WRITE STUFF

To be a successful sportswriter, you will need to develop your writing skills. Writing, of course, is of the utmost

MAKING THE ADJUSTMENT

Although your desire may be to get into a career as a sports journalist, you may find that opportunities are not there. If that's the case, try to get involved with news writing. It might not be exactly what you're looking for, but it will allow you to develop your talent as a writer and as a researcher in a fast-paced environment. Also, because legal issues are such a big part of the sports world these days, you may learn things as a news reporter that will help you when you eventually move to sports.[3]

importance for a sportswriter. The reporter has to write in a clear, concise, and organized way in order to effectively convey the information to the reader. It is also important to develop a "voice" for your writing, which is the tone in which it reads. Even broadcasters have to write much of their own material, too.

COMMUNICATION SKILLS

Although your writing is the final product—what everyone will read—you can't write without getting the information first. That is why it is very important to be good at interacting with others, even if it's not an official interview. Sportswriters rely on all sorts of people for information—the athletes, agents, coaches, team executives—so it is important to have a good rapport with your sources. In an official interview setting, a good interviewer will often get better answers than somebody who is timid or unprepared.

KNOW IT ALL

Today, almost every newspaper has an online counterpart. Many news organizations are only online. That means that writers are often called on to do other tasks, such as taking photos or video, hosting podcasts and online chats, or appearing on newscasts.

"Today, for the most part, if you're going to go into the media, you're not going to just write," said Stark. "If you're a kid in school, you need to be familiar with every platform. Every aspect of the media, every medium, you need to be familiar. You need to make sure you're comfortable with all of them."[4]

CHECKLIST

Is a career as a sportswriter a good fit for you? Discover if you've got what it takes with this checklist.

- *Do you have an interest in sports?*

- *Do you enjoy reading, writing, and public speaking?*

- *Are you able to thrive when working under pressure?*

- *When researching a subject, do you have a thirst for uncovering all angles of that subject?*

If you answered yes to most of these questions, you are well on your way to becoming a sportswriter. If you answered no to most of them, then other sports journalism jobs might be a better fit, such as copy editor or producer.

HOW TO GET THERE

DEVELOP YOUR STYLE

It is never too early to begin developing your writing style. The best way you can improve your writing is to simply keep writing. Many writers also read the work of other writers and try to learn from their writing styles. Stark agreed, saying,

> One of the things I think is important, if you want to be a writer, you pick out your favorite writers and you really read them carefully and you study them and analyze them and think, 'What makes them good?' You teach yourself a lot about writing just by the people you choose to read and how closely you read them.[5]

Stark also suggested that prospective journalists watch television sports broadcasts. "You need to watch *SportsCenter*, and you need to get a feel for what kinds of stories are told and in what kinds of ways. We tell stories at ESPN every possible way you can tell them."[6]

A SIMILAR FIELD

Another option for those who love being around sports and want to be involved with the media is becoming involved as a sports information director or media relations director. Sports information directors and media relations directors work for colleges and professional teams and are involved with the publication of media guides, press releases, and news stories about those teams and schools.[7]

GET PRACTICE

While in high school, get involved with as many forms of media as possible.

Many international events allow reporters access to athletes in a mixed zone. The athletes have to walk through the zone on the way out of the field of play.

While you can develop skills with some high school courses, nothing beats practical experience. If your high school has a newspaper, find out how you can get involved. Some schools also have video, audio, and graphic design or page layout opportunities. Outside of school, Stark suggested that students start blogs or learn how to get involved with podcasts. "If you want to get into media, you need to learn how to do everything. That's the fun of it," he said.[8]

GET A COLLEGE DEGREE—AND EXPERIENCE

After high school, set your sights on obtaining a college degree. And, while you're in college, get more involved with media opportunities through campus newspapers, television stations, and radio stations. If there is a local newspaper in your town, ask about internship opportunities as well.

LOVE SPORTS

"I love my job. I love everything about my job," Stark said. "In the end, what makes people sports fans is they love sports. They love the games, they love the people who play the games. They love to hear and read good stories about teams and people and champions— people who are funny, people who really inspire us because of the challenges they overcome. I still love telling those stories, I still love being at the ballpark, I still love being in a stadium when the home team wins some kind of title to feel the incredible emotion

KEEP YOUR HEAD UP

Breaking into sports journalism can be a difficult process. When an opening at a newspaper or radio or television station does come open, there could be dozens, or even hundreds, of applicants for that one position. Just because you don't get that job, it doesn't mean you aren't cut out for the business. "Finding that first job is always the hardest, but don't get discouraged," sportswriter Jonathan Rand said.[9] Sportscaster Steve Degler advises to never turn down an opportunity to build up your experience. Even if you are asked to do a game or event you don't want to do, do it anyway. "It's a game, and you're getting paid to be there. What could be better?" he said.[10]

It is important for journalists to routinely follow the news so they are kept up-to-date on current events.

of all those thousands of people experiencing that same emotion at once.

"That's why covering sports is still the greatest job on earth. It's why it's the coolest job in the world. Not that there isn't a lot of work—there is—but I often say, 'It's a labor of love, and it's a good thing because there's a lot of labor.'"[11]

GET YOUR FOOT IN THE DOOR

O nce you have chosen a career that you are interested in, there are many ways for you to get started down the path to that career. One of the best ways to learn about that specific career is by reaching out to professionals who have the job you are interested in. Ask them about their job and what you can do to get on track to pursue that career as well.

Job shadowing is a great way to learn about a given career. Shadowing involves spending a day with someone in your field so you can see what he or she does on a daily basis. This can be an eye-opening experience, especially in the sports industry, where the average person is only familiar with what is seen during a competition. Pay close attention to the various tasks the professional takes part in each day, and don't be afraid to ask a lot of questions. However, it is important to be respectful to the person helping you and to remember that he or she likely worked very hard to get to that position.

It is never too early to start getting experience. Any way you can get involved with your chosen field is beneficial. Even if you have to take entry-level positions or unpaid internships, the experience you gain will be valuable as you move forward. At the same time, getting experience in a particular field can also serve as a great opportunity to see if you actually enjoy that line of work. Sometimes a job seems like a perfect fit from the outside, but once you try it out you realize it just isn't for you.

Getting experience can also help you cultivate relationships that could be helpful for career advancement. Networking is especially important in sports careers, which tend to be very competitive. Sell yourself to the people you wish to associate with, and let them know you are willing to do whatever is needed to learn their craft. You don't even have to seek a job when reaching out to potential contacts. Simply making friends and learning about their experiences can help you prepare for your future.

To many people, the sports industry is a glamorous one to work in. That means the careers in sports are often very sought after. With hard work and a lot of passion, anything is possible. However, it is important to remember that there are many opportunities to be involved with sports that don't require having a full-time job in the industry. There are many volunteer and part-time opportunities in coaching, officiating, administrating, and other areas of sports at all levels, from youth sports to professional sports.

PROFESSIONAL ORGANIZATIONS

Here are some professional organizations you might want to contact for more information on the jobs in this book.

PROFESSIONAL ATHLETE

Major League Baseball Players Association
http://mlbplayers.mlb.com

National Basketball Player's Association
www.nbpa.org/

National Football League Players Association
www.nflplayers.com

National Hockey League Players' Association
www.nhlpa.com

SPORTS AGENT

International Management Group
www.imgworld.com

Sports Agent Directory
www.sports-agent-directory.com

Sports Management Worldwide
www.smww.com

COLLEGE COACH

National Association of Intercollegiate Athletics
http://naia.cstv.com

National Collegiate Athletic Association
www.ncaa.org

National Soccer Coaches Association of America
www.nscaa.com

SPORTSWRITER

Associated Press Sports Editors
www.apsportseditors.org

National Association of Broadcasters
www.nab.org

Society of Professional Journalists
www.spj.org

MARKET FACTS

JOB	NUMBER OF JOBS	GROWTH RATE	
Professional Athlete	16,500, but very competitive on the highest level	Much faster than average	
Agent	22,700 (includes agents for athletes and performers)	Much faster than average	
Coach	225,700 (includes scouts; approximately half held part-time jobs)	Much faster than average	
Sportswriter	69,300 (includes news analysts, reporters, and correspondents)	Decline moderately	

MEDIAN WAGE	RELATED JOBS	SKILLS
$40,480	Dietitian or nutritionist, fitness worker, physical therapist	hardworking, passionate, determined, focused
$61,890	Lawyer, manager in other business field	excels in academics, strong negotiator, communication skills
$28,340	Dietitian or nutritionist, recreational therapist, teacher	motivator, people skills, good teacher, passionate, leader
$34,850	Broadcaster, public relations specialist	calmness under pressure, communication skills, research skills

All statistics from the *Bureau of Labor Statistics Occupational Outlook Handbook, 2010–2011 Edition*

GLOSSARY

aesthetic
Having a sense of beauty.

analyze
To examine something critically.

apprentice
A person who works for another to learn a trade.

askance
Looking on someone or something with suspicion or mistrust.

cardiovascular
Pertaining to the heart and blood vessels.

depicting
Showing something visually.

eloquent
Having fluent and appropriate speech.

embellish
To make something beautiful with an ornament or addition.

endorsement
Supporting and representing a product or business.

internship
A program that provides an opportunity for newcomers to gain experience.

lucrative

Very profitable.

median

The midpoint of a range of numbers arranged in order.

negotiate

To bargain with others.

plethora

An excessive amount.

prospective

Having the potential to do or be something.

resilient

Having an ability to bounce back from adversity.

rigorous

Being thorough and exhaustive.

transcend

To rise above or exceed in excellence.

vivid

Strikingly clear.

ADDITIONAL RESOURCES

FURTHER READINGS

Careers in Focus: Coaches & Fitness Professionals. New York: Ferguson, 2008. Print.

Devantier, Alecia T., and Carol A. Turkington. *Extraordinary Jobs in Sports.* New York: J.G. Ferguson, 2007. Print.

Heitzmann, Ray. *Opportunities in Sports and Fitness Careers.* New York: McGraw-Hill, 2003. Print.

WEB LINKS

To learn more about sports jobs, visit ABDO Publishing Company online at **www.abdopublishing.com**. Web sites about sports jobs are featured on our Book Links page. These links are routinely monitored and updated to provide the most current information available.

SOURCE NOTES

CHAPTER 1. IS A SPORTS JOB FOR YOU?

1. "Vol 2, Issue 20: Individual Differences Among Athletes." *sportpsych.unt.edu.* Center for Sport Psychology and Performance Excellence at the University of North Texas, n.d. Web. 24 Aug. 2010.

2. "Jordan's Jumper Secures Chicago's Sixth Title." *NBA Encyclopedia Playoff Edition.* National Basketball Association, n.d. Web. 27 Sept. 2010.

3. Ibid.

4. George F. Will. *Bunts.* New York: Simon, 1999. 50. Print.

5. Gilbert Rogin. "An Odd Sport and an Unusual Champion." *Sports Illustrated,* 18 Oct. 1965. 98–114. Print.

6. Micah Pollens-Dempsey. "The 11 Best Baseball Quotes of All Time." *bleacherreport.com.* Bleacher Report, 30 Aug. 2010. Web. 27 Sept. 2010.

7. "Quotes." *COACHK.com.* COACHK.com, n.d. Web. 27 Sept. 2010.

CHAPTER 2. WHAT IS A PROFESSIONAL ATHLETE?

1. Kurt Badenhausen. "World's Highest-Paid Athletes 2009," *Forbes.com.* Forbes, 10 Aug. 2009. Web. 27 Sept. 2010.

2. "Kody Lostroh." *PBRNow.com.* Professional Bull Riders, Inc., n.d. Web. 27 Sept. 2010.

3. "Professional athlete." *Exploring Career Information from the Bureau of Labor Statistics, 2010-11 Edition.* U.S. Bureau of Labor Statistics, n.d. Web. 27 Sept. 2010.

4. Kevin Youkilis. Personal interview. 23 Jun. 2010.

5. Jonathan Papelbon. Personal Interview. 23 Jun. 2010.

6. Associated Press. "Banged-up Eagles aim to avoid more injuries as preseason games begin." *NFL.com.* NFL Enterprises LLC. 2009. Web. 14 Oct. 2010.

7. Howard Fendrich. "Plenty of pressure on Lindsey Vonn as Olympics approach." *boston.com.* The Boston Globe, 8 Dec. 2009. Web. 27 Sept. 2010.

8. "Professional athlete." *Exploring Career Information from the Bureau of Labor Statistics, 2010-11 Edition.* U.S. Bureau of Labor Statistics, n.d. Web. 27 Sept. 2010.

9. Pablo S. Torre. "How (and Why) Athletes Go Broke." *SI Vault.* Sports Illustrated, 23 Mar. 2009. Web. 27 Sept. 2010.

10. Kevin Youkilis. Personal interview. 23 Jun. 2010.

11. Ibid.

12. Ibid

SOURCE NOTES CONTINUED

13. "NFL Hopeful FAQs." NFLplayers.com. NFL Players Association, n.d. Web. 27 Sept. 2010.

14. "Average Major League Baseball Career 5.6 Years, Says New Study." *Science Daily*. Science Daily, 11 July 2007. Web. 27 Sept. 2010.

CHAPTER 3. WOULD YOU MAKE A GOOD PROFESSIONAL ATHLETE?

1. Kevin Youkilis. Personal interview. 23 Jun. 2010.

2. Ibid.

3. Matt Cronin. "Work pays off for Serena at Wimbledon." *Fox Sports*. Fox Sports Interactive Media, 3 Jul. 2010. Web. 14 Oct. 2010.

4. Derek Jeter. *The Life You Imagine*. New York: Crown, 2000. 21. Print.

5. Jonathan Papelbon. Personal interview. 23 Jun. 2010.

6. Marco Scutaro. Personal interview. 23 Jun. 2010.

7. Alecia T. Devantier and Carol A. Turkington. *Extraordinary Jobs in Sports*. New York: Ferguson, 2007. 19. Print.

8. Marco Scutaro. Personal interview. 23 Jun. 2010.

9. Derek Jeter. *The Life You Imagine*. New York: Crown, 2000. 21. Print.

10. "NFL Hopeful FAQs." *NFLplayers.com*. NFL Players Association, n.d. Web. 27 Sept. 2010.

11. Ibid.

12. Kevin Youkilis. Personal interview. 23 Jun. 2010.

13. Frank Litsky. "Don Hutson, Star Pass-Catcher, Dies at 84." *New York Times*. New York Times Company, 27 June 1997. Web. 14 Oct. 2010.

14. "Willie Mays Quotes." *Baseball Almanac*. Baseball Almanac. n.d. Web. 14 Oct. 2010.

15. Kevin Youkilis. Personal interview. 23 Jun. 2010.

CHAPTER 4. WHAT IS A SPORTS AGENT?

1. "Memorable quotes for *Jerry Maguire*." *IMDb*. The Internet Movie Database, n.d. Web. 27 Sept. 2010.

2. Tom Mills. Personal interview. 14 July 2010.

3. Ibid.

4. "Sports Agent Directory." *Sports Agent Directory*. Sports Agent Director, n.d. Web. 27 Sept. 2010.

5. Tom Mills. Personal interview. 14 July 2010.

6. Alecia T. Devantier and Carol A. Turkington. *Extraordinary Jobs in Sports*. New York: Ferguson, 2007. 75–76. Print.

7. Tom Mills. Personal interview. 14 July 2010.

8. Alecia T. Devantier and Carol A. Turkington. *Extraordinary Jobs in Sports*. New York: Ferguson, 2007. 76. Print.

9. Tom Mills. Personal interview. 14 July 2010.

10. "A Career as a Sports Agent." *Top End Sports*. Top End Sports, 27 Dec. 2009. Web. 27 Sept. 2010.

11. "Sports Agent Salary." *Become a Sports Agent*. Become a Sports Agent, n.d. Web. 27 Sept. 2010.

12. Tom Mills. Personal interview. 14 July 2010.

13. "Sports Agent: Career Definition, Occupational Outlook, and Education Prerequisites." *DegreeDirectory.org*. DegreeDirectory.org, n.d. Web. 27 Sept. 2010.

CHAPTER 5. WOULD YOU MAKE A GOOD SPORTS AGENT?

1. Alecia T. Devantier and Carol A. Turkington. *Extraordinary Jobs in Sports*. New York: Ferguson, 2007. 76. Print.

2. Tom Mills. Personal interview. 14 July 2010.

3. Ibid.

4. Ray Heitzmann. *Opportunities in Sports and Fitness Careers*. Chicago: VGM Career Books, 2003. 155. Print.

5. Alecia T. Devantier and Carol A. Turkington. *Extraordinary Jobs in Sports*. New York: Ferguson, 2007. 74. Print.

6. Tom Mills. Personal interview. 14 July 2010.

7. Ibid.

8. Alecia T. Devantier and Carol A. Turkington. *Extraordinary Jobs in Sports*. New York: Ferguson, 2007. 77. Print.

9. Tom Mills. Personal interview. 14 July 2010.

10. Ibid.

CHAPTER 6. WHAT IS A COLLEGE COACH?

1. "Interview: Mike Krzyzewski Collegiate Basketball Champion." *Academy of Achievement*. American Academy of Achievement, 22 May 1997. Web. 14 Oct. 2010.

2. Bureau of Labor Statistics. "Athletes, Coaches, Umpires, and Related Workers." *Occupational Outlook Handbook, 2010–11 Edition*. U.S. Department of Labor. 17 Dec. 2010. Web. 27 Sept. 2010.

SOURCE NOTES CONTINUED

3. David Leon Moore. "Pete Carroll goes to Seahawks, leaves questions behind at USC." *USAToday.com*. USA Today, 12 Jan. 2010. Web. 27 Sept. 2010.

4. Barry Hinson. Personal interview. 14 July 2010.

5. Ibid.

6. Ibid.

7. Ibid.

8. Ibid.

9. Bureau of Labor Statistics. "Athletes, Coaches, Umpires, and Related Workers." *Occupational Outlook Handbook, 2010–11 Edition*. U.S. Department of Labor. 17 Dec. 2010. Web. 27 Sept. 2010.

10. "University of Colorado Athletic Department Directory." *CUBuffs.com*. University of Colorado Athletics, n.d. 27 Sept. 2010.

11. "Athletic Staff Directory." *Broncbusters Athletics*. Garden City Community College, n.d. Web. 27 Sept. 2010.

12. "US Colleges and Universities." BrainTrack. FutureMeld LLC, n.d. Web. 27 Sept. 2010.

13. "Quotes." *COACHK.com*. COACHK.com, n.d. Web. 27 Sept. 2010.

14. Barry Hinson. Personal interview. 14 July 2010.

CHAPTER 7. WOULD YOU MAKE A GOOD COLLEGE COACH?

1. "Quotes." *COACHK.com*. COACHK.com, n.d. Web. 27 Sept. 2010.

2. Barry Hinson. Personal interview. 14 July 2010.

3. Ibid.

4. Ibid.

5. Ibid.

6. Frank Litsky and John Branch. "John Wooden, Who Built Incomparable Dynasty at U.C.L.A., Dies at 99." *New York Times*. New York Times Company, 4 June 2010. Web. 14 Oct. 2010.

7. Barry Hinson. Personal interview. 14 July 2010.

8. "Sherri Coale." *soonersports.com*. University of Oklahoma Athletics, n.d. Web. 27 Sept. 2010.

9. Barry Hinson. Personal interview. 14 July 2010.

CHAPTER 8. WHAT IS A SPORTSWRITER?

1. "Salary Snapshot for Journalist Job." *PayScale*. PayScale, Inc., 25 Sept. 2010. Web. 27 Sept. 2010.

2. Stephanie Chen. "Newspapers fold as readers defect and economy sours." *CNN.com*. Cable News Network, n.d. Web. 27 Sept. 2010.

3. Michael Mandel. "The Journalism Job Market: Part I, Looking Back." *Bloomberg Businessweek*. Bloomberg LP, 16 Sept. 2009. Web. 27 Sept. 2010.

4. Jayson Stark. Personal Interview. 14 July 2010.

5. Ibid.

6. Ibid.

7. Ibid.

CHAPTER 9. WOULD YOU MAKE A GOOD SPORTSWRITER?

1. Alecia T. Devantier and Carol A. Turkington. *Extraordinary Jobs in Sports*. New York: Ferguson, 2007. 101. Print.

2. Ibid. 99.

3. Jayson Stark. Personal Interview. 14 July 2010.

4. Ibid.

5. Ray Heitzmann. *Opportunities in Sports and Fitness Careers*. New York: McGraw, 2003. 61. Print.

6. Jayson Stark. Personal Interview. 14 July 2010.

7. Alecia T. Devantier and Carol A. Turkington. *Extraordinary Jobs in Sports*. New York: Ferguson, 2007. 83. Print.

8. Jayson Stark. Personal Interview. 14 July 2010.

9. Alecia T. Devantier and Carol A. Turkington. *Extraordinary Jobs in Sports*. New York: Ferguson, 2007. 102. Print.

10. Ibid. 82.

11. Jayson Stark. Personal Interview. 14 July 2010.

INDEX

ABOUT THE AUTHOR

Brian Howell has been a sports journalist for more than 17 years, writing about high school, college, and professional athletics. He has been a beat reporter covering the Colorado Rockies and the Denver Broncos while earning several writing awards during his career. He has also had books published about the Atlanta Braves, Colorado Rockies, Denver Broncos, New Orleans Saints, New York Yankees, and Oakland Athletics. A native of Colorado, he lives with his wife and four children in Denver.

PHOTO CREDITS